Porcupines

Victoria Blakemore

© 2019 Victoria Blakemore

All rights reserved. This book or parts thereof may not be reproduced in any form, stored in any retrieval system, or transmitted in any form by any means—electronic, mechanical, photocopy, recording, or otherwise—without prior written permission of the publisher, except as provided by United States of America copyright law. For permission requests, write to the publisher, at "Attention: Permissions Coordinator," at the address below.

vblakemore.author@gmail.com

Copyright info/picture credits

Cover, Harald/AdobeStock; Page 3, leswhalley/Pixabay; Page 5, Mani300/Pixabay; Page 7, Dennis/AdobeStock; Page 9, bodnarinq/Adobestock; Page 11, Suju/Pixabay; Pages 12-13, Kapa65/Pixabay; Page 15, jimcumming88/AdobeStock; Page 17, Lena721/Pixabay; Page 19, Bernell/Pixabay; Page 21, outdoorsman/Shutterstock; Page 23; kajomyot/AdobeStock; Page 25, Mircea Costina/AdobeStock; Page 27, Mgarlock/Pixabay; Page 29, Alexandra_Koch/Pixabay; Page 31, Bernell/Pixabay; Page 33, Harald/AdobeStock

Table of Contents

What are Porcupines? 2

Size 4

Physical Characteristics 6

Quills 8

Habitat 10

Range 12

Diet 14

Communication 16

Movement 18

Porcupettes 20

Porcupine Life 22

Predators 24

Population 26

Porcupines in Danger 28

Helping Porcupines 30

Glossary 34

What Are Porcupines?

Porcupines are small mammals. They are members of the rodent family. Some other members of the rodent family are rats, mice, and squirrels.

There are twenty-nine different kinds of porcupines. They differ in size, color, and where they live.

The word porcupine comes from the Latin roots "porcus," which means pig, and "spina," which means thorns. So the meaning of the word porcupine is thorn pig.

Size

Different kinds of porcupines grow to be different sizes. The smallest porcupines grow to be about fifteen inches long. The largest grow to be about three feet long.

When fully grown, porcupines can weigh between two and seventy-seven pounds.

Male porcupines are often larger than female porcupines.

Physical Characteristics

Porcupines are black, brown, gray, and white in color. They use their color as **camouflage**. It helps them to blend in to their habitat.

They have a greasy coating on their bodies. It is thought to keep them from getting an infection if they get poked by a quill.

Some porcupines have **hollow** quills on their tails. They rattle when they are shaken. The sound is used as a warning to other animals.

Quills

Porcupines are the only kind of rodent that has quills. Their quills are sharp spines that stick out of their body. Their quills keep them safe from **predators**.

Porcupines can have up to 30,000 quills. They grow new quills to replace any they lose.

Their quills come in different colors and sizes. They are all sharp and can get stuck in your skin if you touch the points.

Habitat

Porcupines are usually found in forests and grasslands. They prefer areas with lots of plants so they can find enough food.

Some porcupines may also be found in rocky deserts. They are able to **adapt** to living in different habitats as long as there are enough plants to eat.

Range

Porcupines are found in many parts of the world. They can be found in Africa, Asia, Europe, and the Americas.

Porcupines are found in countries such as Brazil, Canada, the United States, India, England, and South Africa.

Diet

Porcupines are **herbivores**. They only eat plants.

In the winter, porcupines often eat tree bark and evergreen needles. When it is warmer, more food is available. They eat fruit, leaves, grasses, roots, and stems.

Porcupines have large front teeth that allow them to **gnaw** on their food.

Communication

Porcupines use sound, scent, and touch to communicate. They often rub noses or paws as a greeting.

They make sounds such as grunts, shrieks, and tooth chattering. The sounds can be used as a warning or to **attract** other porcupines.

Porcupines have a scent that they use to mark their **territory**. It tells other porcupines to stay away.

Movement

Porcupines are slow-moving. The fastest a porcupine has been seen running is about two miles per hour.

Porcupines are good at swimming and climbing. They can climb trees to find food. They sometimes build nests in trees.

When climbing, porcupines use their sharp claws to hold on to branches. Their tail can be used to help them balance.

Porcupettes

Porcupines have up to four babies in a **litter**. They are called porcupettes or pups. They are often born in the spring or summer.

When porcupettes are first born their quills are soft. They harden after a few hours.

They can feed themselves when they are about two months old. They often leave their mother around that time.

Porcupine Life

Porcupines are usually **solitary**. They spend most of their time alone. Groups of porcupines are usually made up of a mother and her young. These groups are called prickles.

Some porcupines nest in trees. Others prefer to stay on the ground.

Porcupines are **nocturnal**. They are most active at night. They spend their nights looking for food.

Predators

Although they have sharp quills, porcupines do have several **predators**. In Africa, their main predators are lions and other large cats.

In other parts of the world, animals such as eagles, great-horned owls, martens, and pythons hunt porcupines.

Fishers are related to weasels. They are able to catch porcupines and flip them over without touching their quills.

Population

Most porcupines are **stable** in the wild. Their populations are not in trouble. Almost all kinds of porcupines are listed as **least concern**.

There are a few kinds that are **vulnerable**. They could become **endangered** if their populations continue to **decline**.

In the wild, porcupines often live up to seven years. Some have lived nearly twenty years.

Porcupines in Danger

In some areas, porcupines are hunted and killed by people. They eat plants, so many people think of them as pests.

They are also hunted for their quills and meat. In some parts of the world, porcupine quills are thought to bring good luck.

Porcupine habitats are being destroyed for farms, buildings, and roads.

Helping Porcupines

In some places, special areas of protected land have been set up. They provide animals like porcupines with a safe habitat.

Groups like the African Wildlife Foundation are working to set up more protected areas. They want to protect animals like porcupines.

Some countries have made it **illegal** to catch and remove wild porcupines.

Some groups focus on education. They work with farmers to come up with ways to keep their crops safe from porcupines. They also provide **incentives** for farmers who use these methods.

Glossary

Adapt: to change

Attract: to cause to come near

Camouflage: using color to blend in to the surroundings

Decline: get smaller

Endangered: at risk of becoming extinct

Gnaw: to bite on or chew again and again

Herbivore: an animal that eats only plants

Hollow: having an empty space inside

Illegal: against the law

Incentive: something that makes a person want to do something

Least concern: not likely to become endangered

Litter: a group of animals born at the same time

Nocturnal: animals that are active at night

Predator: an animal that hunts other animals for food

Solitary: living alone

Stable: unchanging

Territory: an area of land that an animal clams as its own

Vulnerable: an animal that could soon become endangered

About the Author

Victoria Blakemore is a first grade teacher in Southwest Florida with a passion for reading.

You can visit her at

www.enchantedinelementary.com

Also in This Series

Also in This Series

www.ingramcontent.com/pod-product-compliance
Lightning Source LLC
Chambersburg PA
CBHW040221040426
42333CB00049B/3187